Poems For The Year 2020

POEMS FOR THE YEAR 2020

Eighty poets on the pandemic

EDITED BY MERRYN WILLIAMS

All rights reserved. No part of this work covered by the copyright herein may be reproduced or used in any means – graphic, electronic, or mechanical, including copying, recording, taping, or information storage and retrieval systems – without written permission of the publisher.

Printed by imprintdigital
Upton Pyne, Exeter
www.digital.imprint.co.uk

Typesetting by The Book Typesetters
us@thebooktypesetters.com
07422 598 168
www.thebooktypesetters.com

Cover design by Rosalind Evans
ros.evans@protonmail.com

Published by Shoestring Press
19 Devonshire Avenue, Beeston, Nottingham, NG9 1BS
(0115) 925 1827
www.shoestringpress.co.uk

First published 2021
© Copyright: Individual poets
© Cover image: Rosalind Evans

The moral rights of the authors have been asserted.

ISBN 978-1-912524-90-7

in memory of Dr Li Wenliang
1985–2020

INTRODUCTION

The year 2020, like the years 1066 and 1914, will be remembered for one thing only; indeed will be remembered for centuries if the human race survives. All the poems in this anthology were written in the plague year.

Other generations have suffered other plagues and have described them. Thomas Nashe, for instance, in 1593, was as aware of mortality as we have all had to become:

Brightness falls from the air;
Queens have died young and fair;
Dust hath closed Helen's eye;
I am sick, I must die.
Lord have mercy on us!

Thousands upon thousands of plague poems in various languages have been written in 2020, and some of these poems will be imperishable. I thought it was important to collect the best ones I could find before we start talking about something else.

Other people had the same idea. Janine Booth put together a little book, *CoronaVerses: Poems from the Pandemic*, as early as April 2020. Manchester Metropolitan University produced a vast online anthology, 'Write where we are now'. I raided both of them, found some wonderful pieces, and also sent out a general appeal for poems about any aspect of corona virus and the lockdowns. I received many more than I could use, from five continents and from all corners of Britain, and am really sorry that so many good poems had to be left out. There are probably many more again that I haven't seen.

My aim was to cover all possible angles of the Situation. Each person's experience is slightly different, as illustrated by Matt Black in 'Down our street', and I didn't want too many poems about being stuck indoors feeling bored, or too much doom and gloom. Subjects include sickening from Covid, bereavement from Covid, the 'other dead' (I lost friends from other causes in the same year), deserted cities, separation from spouses and children, masks, social distancing, 'Thought for the Day', animals invading the street, deep appreciation of our key workers and a deep distrust for politicians.

There are also poems which celebrate human resourcefulness. People cultivate their gardens, exchange pictures, rediscover old books, try out new recipes and observe birds. A grandmother cheerfully goes out to pick the 2020 harvest and ninety-year-old Meg Peacocke gives two thoughtless young men a piece of her mind. We are so much luckier than our ancestors. We can communicate through words and images, and, as I write, the vaccines are being rolled out.

The cover image was inspired by Deborah Maccoby's poem 'Violet Carpenter Bee'. While this crisis is obsessing us, we remain aware of the wider threat to the planet, and the useful little bee, 'essential worker for humanity', is a symbol of hope.

So, this slim volume contains some magnificent work. In the words of the American Gail Holst-Warhaft, quoting Pericles in 'Athens 430 BC':

Just realise
that the Spartans will go, plague will pass –
you'll still be citizens of a great city.

MERRYN WILLIAMS

In the Beginning: China, South Africa

BY DEGREES

The security guard puts the gun to my head
then clicks. He turns it to show me: 36 degrees

and waves me in, his expression hidden
behind his mask, his eyes vacant.

I walk around the almost empty supermarket.
No eggs, no veg, the milk sold out, less pasta

than three days ago. Chinese New Year music
still plays on the store's radio, its merriness

like a slap. People queue up rather than use self-service,
nervous to touch what others have touched.

Heading back I see my apartment is sealed off.
I must walk round the back, to the other entrance

guarded now by five policemen with temperature guns.
I go in and they scan me again: 37 degrees.

Other cities don't have it like this.
Going out like this is a privilege.

DAVID TAIT, Shanghai, China: 2 February 2020

GESTATION

March 2020

Sure as babies,
nine months down the line
there'll be a boom
of virus poems.

No one will ask
*Do you remember
what you were doing when…?*
because we'll all know:

the wailing and teething,
the semantic nappy-changing
will be quite
unmistakable.

HARRY OWEN, Grahamstown, South Africa

Rest of the World

Mary had a little bug
The one they call Corona
She caught it at a Catch-up
Wi her pals, Yvette and Shona.
Who else was there?
"I dinnae care:
We've no been oot fur weeks"
Now Shona's blue, in ITU,
Too breathless when she speaks.

Mary had a little cough
She didnae wear a mask
Instead she wore a sticker
Saying "I'm exempt, don't ask"
Coughing in the kitchen
As she plated up the scones,
Then a round of filtered selfies
Using all The Girls i-phones.

Mary had a little bug
And now so does her Granny,
Her boss, her son,
His pal, his mum
'Cos Mary is a fanny.

ANON, Scotland

DRIVING

That summer we kept quiet in cars.
My father hated driving and required silence,
so that summer, on short journeys, on motorways

on the backseat, we watched our mouths.
At the same time, the elm trees were dying
and ours, the shade-giving mighty elm,

quietly ferried the beetle's parasite into its bark.
Its leaves flagged and yellowed, eccentric patterns
scarring the trunk. So many trees died, starved

quickly after the beetles first visit, ours went in
a single summer, unnoticed by us, then felled
for safety soon after. By the time I was driving I

heard they were breeding elite elms that might
resist the pathogens. How carefully I drive now,
so like my father, yet shame when it returns

is powder-light, yet heavy as logs, where there's
a sharp smell of foxes and a beetle is busy
in the twig-crotch scratching out its wretched sound.

MONA ARSHI, Under the shade of the Indian Bean Tree, Ealing

BETJEMANIA

Confession in the time of Coronavirus

The sort of girls I like to see
Are nowadays too young for me.
Gosh, skimpy tops! Phew, lycra'd thighs!
That's too much flesh for my weak eyes.

These sirens with their well-toned tums,
Some with daughters, some with chums
Go jogging past in careless chatter,
Ignoring us, the slow and fatter

Who shrink against the prickly hedge
Or teeter on the pavement's edge.
These gaily call, but not to me:
I'm short of breath, and weak of knee.

O staunch Myfanwy, sporty Pam,
Joan Hunter-Dunn, how sad I am
That you, my long-gone loves, have faded
From memory now; but, old and jaded

Though I be, I'll confess I'm grateful to
These lithe athletic ladies who,
With iPhones, headphones, glowing cheeks,
Have brightened so my lockdown weeks.

ADRIAN BARLOW, Cheltenham

ODDS

My diary tells me what I would have done
if someone had not caught a pangolin
and sold it at a market in Wuhan -
the theatres, classes, cafes I'd be in
and am not, now I'm stranded here at home.

Few people on the streets. They come and go,
among them, some of those who might have died
in accidents by air, or sea, or road
or skirmishes in clubs or streets at night,
but are not dead - live on, and never know.

And lovers too, who might by chance have met
by watercooler, bus stop, or in bars
now swiping lonely on the internet
have missed a romance written in the stars -
and never know they've something to regret.

But when my diary ceases to record
the things I would have done, what might have been,
the dual versions of what is in store
will end – the one we've lost will, like a dream
just fade away, unknown and unexplored.

MEG BARTON, Oxford

PICTURES

Easter Sunday 12th April 2020

My son sends me a picture
of a simnel cake
he has baked this Easter,
that we cannot share.
My daughter sends me a scene
from her balcony
full of red tulips
she has grown from seed –

and I carry these images
in my heart.
The fluency of their fingers
more precious than prayer.

DENISE BENNETT, Havant, Hampshire.

DOWN OUR STREET

Roshan and Aisha make lots of cups of tea, stick to new daily routines created to maintain cheer. They stare out of the window. They want chocolate bars which they are too scared to go and buy.

Josh, who never had the courage to leave the computer job he hates, and has always longed for an alternative lifestyle, has dug up his small back garden and plants spinach and garlic to bolster his immune system.

Wojcek is desperate to get back to Poland, to see his family, but is worried that if he gets there he will never be allowed to return. He drinks 4 cans of strong lager, starting at 6, every evening.

Liz weaves bright new futures in her mind, of a world that has learnt its lessons, and looks forward to the autumn. She sews scrub bags for the NHS, plans to make recycled masks, knit rainbows.

Jade can't get her usual supply of methodone, but has found some cheap spice. She likes the sunshine. Although she is hungry, she's got the gang, and her lockdown is flying by.

Stephen, aged 75, cupboards overflowing with cheese, ready meals and whisky, thinks it is Xmas. He Facetimes his son every evening at half past six. Eats and drinks like there is no tomorrow.

Lorraine spends 10 hours a day on Facebook campaigning for the cure of Covid 19 by a combination of turmeric teas and yogic breathing.

Rob develops business plans for using the last reserves from his bankrupt cafe business, and some thin Government support, for a start-up in developing video games – his teenage passion. He is in discussions with his landlord about unpaid rent.

Chris and Kerri lie in bed every morning, rowing over how much screen time Ben and Gemma, aged 8 and 6, should have every day. Ben and Gemma are downstairs creating alternative worlds in Minecraft.

Alexandra texts Gilly that a G and T at 5 tonight in the back garden, with 6 feet between them, will be completely fine, surely darling.

John is alone in his flat, sweating in bed, waiting for his twice-weekly call from an NHS volunteer telephone befriender.

Louisa bleaches the front letter box, the front door bell, the wing mirrors of her Citroen Picasso, every morning at 7am.

Rashida has spent 2 days weeping for her Mum, who died aged 52, for lack of PPE. She is also a nurse, goes back to work tomorrow.

Mike eats Monster Munch and reads online conspiracy theories and analysis that show that Covid19 is a statistical myth created by capitalists to increase global control over consumer populations.

Melanie, asthmatic, wakes up thinking she has Covid every morning. She spends her days on Facebook looking for posts that will offer her lifelines for her more precarious than ever mental health.

Jane is on 80% furlough, and now she can no longer go to restaurants or on holiday, is better off than when she was working. She reads, rings friends, listens to Guardian recommended Spotify lists. She loves lockdown, but knows it is not right to say it.

Ashley clings to the wreckage of S.S. Hope, stares across the grey, choppy sea.

Unwittingly, and despite best efforts, the small corner shop spreads Covid 19.

The pub is closed.

The pigeons coo-coo, coo-coo.

Callum, aged 4, draws pictures of giants every day. He loves his Mum and Dad at home together for this spring that seems to last forever.

MATT BLACK, Leamington Spa

HANCOCK'S HALF HOUR

Broadcast at five o'clock
to millions of eager viewers

Our hapless hero
tackles the latest crisis

Trying to sound authoritative
but never quite in control

His spivvy mate
usually gets the better of him

It's not Railway Cuttings
it's Downing Street

It's a situation
but it's not comedy

JANINE BOOTH, Lewes

THE TRAIN

The Russian train has two young women guides,
Katya, slim Helen. Flowered shirt-cloth hides
paunches on the young Mafia. Knives slide
all day on the potato-peeler's knee
between compartments. Sacha grins, strides past,
six feet of engineer. Steam-whistles blast.
The quiet, helpful man who boarded last,
with fluent German, may be KGB.

We saw the wooden towns. We glimpse a moose,
churches with incense, dead pools like a bruise
by slender broken birches. Who would choose
to live here? Fresh food for her child to eat
is Helen's aim. Why, on the final day
do sobs shake her small breasts, to the train's sway?
Sasha, shrunk suddenly, stows tools away
before he meets the murderous Moscow street.

***

Sickness. Each night I board, in home-locked dream,
a fearful train. A boy in bundled green
who has no papers, leaps out, rolls down scree,
races past startled cows. The wet glass streams,
I grip my silvered strip of pills. I know
I must find the young girl, whose vivid glow
means fever. Calm, awake, would I do so?
I doubt it. We are better in our dreams.

I wake, then shiver. The March light blows wild.
How many died? How old is Helen's child?
I must feed cats, next, count the tinned peas, piled
against our hungers, the forgotten rain.
I could use Sacha's tools. Who will bring pills?
In each room sleepers wake, while pure sun spills.
The radio leaks facts. The kettle fills.
Rocked deeper, scared, we still must ride this train.

                        ALISON BRACKENBURY, Cheltenham

BLURRED VISION

We are a child in a car, a man with blurred vision
behind the wheel, taking us for a spin
to see if we crash. He says we can take
our seatbelt off, but even a four-year-old can see
the car is still.in motion. We get out
in a town with a castle, but the castle
is more a name than anything, the castle
is poorly maintained and crumbling, like a big slice
of Cheshire cheese. Now we are in the woods,
trying to focus on the bluebells, visible to the public
in the distance, but still on private land. We travelled
260 miles to get here. The people supposed to be
looking after us drove with a fever, a continuous cough.
They had lost their sense of smell. They did not stop
to go to the toilet. Not even once, they say,
so that means they are still full of shit. Where will we be
in two months' time? Maybe we will be in a rose garden.
Maybe we will still be wearing a mask.
Maybe we will be on a ventilator.
Maybe we will be in a body bag.
Maybe we will still be in the same position,
insisting we did nothing wrong.

MELANIE BRANTON, Weston-super-Mare

YORK

I am the market-place,
no-one comes near me now,
only the rats who scrabble
for the last traces
of bread and fruit,
meat and fish, the cheeses
I once groaned with

I am a snickelway,
everyone is afraid to cut
between my walls,
the gap is so narrow;
I even smell different
though I cling to
lingering odours
of chip butties and piss
and curry in a drain

I am the city walls,
you would not believe
how lonely I am
without your feet
scuffing my stones,
your voices echoing
a thousand tongues.
I loop around the houses
you rarely leave

I am the Minster,
my massive doors
locked. Inside
my empty nave
I grieve, my still bells
toll, silent and grave,
ghost voices ring
from my beams.

On that grotesque
with his mute scream,
a peregrine tears
apart a pigeon's wing

I am the shops
where sad mannequins
in dark windows
reach out stiff arms
to a street
even the homeless
have deserted
where only a fox
is window-shopping

I am the station
with no passengers,
my words fall into silence
The train on Platform 3
Mind the gap
The delayed 13.46
In my ticket hall
among the begonias
a greylag goose
sits on four warm eggs.
I wait and wait
for them to hatch

I am Clifford's Tower,
a child's drawing
of a castle,
so isolated
here on my mound,
looking down on
empty carpark,
deserted streets,

buses that go round
with no people in them
while long-lost voices
clamour inside me

I am the river,
cold and cruel,
if I feel like spilling into
the city I will,
if I feel like swallowing
its desperate young
I'll do that too
and the soldier
who tries to swim across
and the student
stumbling home,
come closer, I will carry you,
I will carry you all the way
to the sea.

CAROLE BROMLEY, York

FOR MY DAUGHTER'S MOTHER-IN-LAW'S SISTER

For my daughter's mother-in-law's sister
is a splendid specimen of woman, lady
of a certain age, not old enough
to be at risk, not at leisure and so,
alas, furloughed.

For my daughter's mother-in-law's sister
is fine in style and substance, efficient,
proficient in many areas. No shirker. She is
a grandmother, and she keeps a flat in Hove
with a view
of the promenade.

For my daughter's mother-in-law's sister,
deskbound for decades, now footloose, fancy-free
but for how long? She has signed an official piece
of paper. Latter-day land girl, she must
make ready, hold steady, join willing ranks
who'll plug the labour gaps
this summer.

For my daughter's mother-in-law's sister
will be a classy fruit picker, in eyeliner,
bright blue, in cropped white linen slacks, a panama hat,
red painted toenails, practical walking sandals.
Decrees say she is needed: she must dirty her hands
for the good of queen
and country.

For my daughter's mother-in-law's sister
must go down to the fields, a trug just hung
carelessly at her elbow. No shirker -
she's a wonderful worker. She will toil
and labour and save the day -
this year's harvest.

My daughter's mother-in-law's sister.

SIMONE MANSELL BROOME, Ceredigion

THE OTHER DEAD

for my late friends Nick Allen, Lorna Barr, and Elizabeth Dawson-Bowling

In Brussels, the Musée des Beaux Arts is closed
until Quasimodo Sunday – some hopes.
Across the world, marinas crammed with
expensive, delicate boats are off-limits
to irresponsible parties. The aged especially
are barred from gathering in expectation
of nativities, miraculous or otherwise.
Few children are out there skating
in either hemisphere, but all are on thin ice.
As for torturers, they must find social distancing
a hindrance even from horseback. The labourer
still stands to the plough, the shepherd
at the fold, but for how much longer?
If they turn away from all other deaths
it is not because they have none themselves.
Yet for those who suffer ineligible loss
from causes that were not the plague
let neither sunshine nor the turning
of the stars dare plead necessity
to mitigate the cruelty of the times.

RIP BULKELEY, Oxford

THE REPAIR SHOP

All our locked-down days they strolled
up the familiar path, pilgrims cradling
broken offerings: harmonium, rocking horse,
steam engine, vase, laying them carefully
on the altar of the priests and priestesses
with the power to touch the chipped,
the stopped, the stained, the shattered
and return them to the untarnished
wholeness of the past – its scarlet and gold,
purple and greenwood, its smooth-wheeled
motion, music-box chimes and peals,
wafts of coal-tar soap, pipe tobacco,
lavender-scented aunts – winding back
the clockwork of the generations
with painstaking, nimble-fingered magic.
And we, the hungry-eyed, watch for a sign
that our splintered world could be restored
by someone with the skill and patience,
the paint, glue, solder or stitch to repair time,
to return us to the days before the age of touch
slammed shut in our astonished faces.

MAGGIE BUTT, London

THE VIRUS

They will not last, the quiet afternoons,
I know that. A beer in the pub garden,
The last mowing of the domestic lawns
And each tree cutting feeling more wooden.

Except that now a virus in the land
Is cancelling the markets and the song.
People in streets have no money to lend
And no ribbons on gifts but only string.

So these are the days to walk through softly,
Wearing masks where stooping people gather,
Leaving out words or else talking gruffly,
Hearing one word but wishing another.

Streets are empty, the cars in garages,
And some take the hit their neighbour dodges.

IAN CAWS, Sussex

EASTER 2020

We are earning our page in World History.
Evenings of empty silence in the streets,
a fox crossing a car park, takeaway in her teeth.
Mornings of spaced-out people in supermarket chains –
even our trolleys might be lethal.
Afternoons of taunting sunshine,
cherry blossom escaping along gutters
where cars sleep on their wheels.
Nature's smile seems sinister
like that phone call in the night.
Pigeons repeat from the trees –
how sad you are/ how lost you are ….
We are earning our page in World History
or a chapter, crammed cold with statistics.

GLADYS MARY COLES, Wirral

LOCKED DOWN

Saltless disappointment at the fingertips
as spinning rings roar for an audience
of earless angels,

an old photograph lies behind the glass:
never such innocence again,
(but you can keep the frame).

DEBORAH COX, Frodsham

IN THE FORTY-FIRST YEAR OF OUR MARRIAGE

we sleep in separate rooms
on separate floors,
use separate bathrooms.

There is only one living room
which at the moment
is exclusively yours.

How to disinfect soft furnishings?
We take turns to use
the single kitchen, and swab

all surfaces before and after.
We hear each other often
calling from our parallel worlds.

The cat, confused, goes from one
to the other with affection
or infection, quite possibly both.

How distant our ruby weekend
now seems — an expensive hotel
in Bath, with staff who,

knowing the occasion,
plied champagne and chocolate.
How we walked hand in hand

along Georgian terraces
amidst careless crowds
breathing the same air.

How long ago it was that we dared
to touch, to feel our skins flex
and merge as if we were one.

And I am grateful for survival,
even yours. We have surrendered
our freedoms for this.

BARBARA CUMBERS, London

LAST WALK AT LYDSTEP

The village is locked-down
but only I can tell tonight, I'm the only
witness to the dark, still lane and the closed pub.
From across the fields I can hear the sea.

Lights glow in a few homes, but the swings
and tennis nets at Celtic Haven Holidays
are slack and unused, the freshly painted
houses and stable blocks will be empty this season.

The place had been a turkey farm which supplied the *QE2*
and my mother; each Christmas for two decades
she'd drive up to us with a bird on the back seat.
Mum died years back and the house sale's going through.

Eleven years ago to the week, Withybush Hospital,
in her ninety-first year. As it should be.
Her heart gave out as ours dare not do
with the hospitals full to breaking now.

So many stars tonight in a perfect, black sky
that brings light from dead worlds and past times.
And stars at my feet – the first flush of wild garlic
with its fresh stink of sweet/sour breath

announcing the cruellest month.
My aunt Annie, the Pembrokeshire charmer,
would have been out foraging and wrenching them up
to gather the bulbs for potions and cures.

Warts, agues and women's troubles: for pennies
she ministered to family and neighbours.
A farm girl before the First War, the plague of 'Nineteen,
then an ex-soldier's wife, a smallholding near Kilgetty.

There's the Plough, Orion's Belt, the North Star,
and countless others I don't recognise.
No winking lights from the transatlantic planes,
now we are shrinking into ourselves, cancelled flights,

the world curling back into itself
for safety, and in fear.
This is the reckoning point, the date,
all manner of events and lives will be defined by this year.

Though the fields at the back of us are newly ploughed,
a flurry of gulls and crows jabbing at the fresh worms;
this afternoon there were hens let loose and scattered
across the empty road. One perched on our wall.

This county's a long way from anywhere,
and closed to visitors now: the police run checks.
Our Headland's been an Iron Age promontory fort,
a narrow strip to defend with the sea at your back.

In the war mum's friend Reg had held a rope
over the edge near Whitesheet Rock above the crashing sea
for school mates to raid the crevice nests for gulls' eggs.
'Big and rich, but tasting of fish. Still, we was so hungry.'

TONY CURTIS, Barry Island

DONCASTER

Boris announced his virus-fix.
Confine yourselves to groups of six.
Surround yourself with social space
and wrap a mask around your face.
This is the sensible solution
to the dispersion of pollution.
This regimen is fair, though tough –
and… Monday will be soon enough.

But lovers of the sport of kings
have other ways to look at things.
No need to ask "why the long face?"
We have been given four days' grace
to gather at the Town Moor Course
and whoop and yell, each to his horse.
Not quite as many as before
but still considerably more
than six. Let us lift up our hearts
before the proper lockdown starts.

And later we'll go on the lam
just like we did at Chelten-ham.
We'll leave the track and hit the boozers
to let the winners treat the losers.
Before we're forced to give a list
of contacts, let's get proudly pissed
and leave our calling-cards around
where they'll be certain to be found.
Come – let us be ubiquitous!

Holy Saint Leger, pray for us…

                                                    ANN DRYSDALE, Gwent

THREADS

for my son, Silas, NHS anaesthetist and rock-climber

Dangling on a rope
hung from a cliff-top
you look like a tiny spider

spinning a thread
the slightest gust
could snap.

Now your patients
are hanging on threads.
And all of you

working on wards
where a terrible
scissor-wielding hag

decides who to spare,
which thread
next to cut.

VICKI FEAVER, South Lanarkshire

EMERGENCY POWERS

You see them get that feeling in their bones
that in a crisis, nothing holds them back.
The gloves are off, constraints do not apply.
That blue lake up near Buxton? Paint it black
(a tribute, maybe, to the Rolling Stones?)
and drive the vermin back to quarantine.

Orban assures Hungarian MPs
he needs more power to beat Covid 19.
The battered opposition, on their knees,
say that should be reviewed. Orban says no.

We have been here before. Back in the dark
of 9/11 Bush said "don't ask why";
torched civil liberties, and lit the spark –
Afghanistan, Iraq, Guantanamo.

PAUL FRANCIS, Shropshire

EVERYONE'S HEARTS WERE CLAPPING

Everyone stood outside their front door.
As the clock struck eight, they began to clap,
slowly, as if someone was coming on stage;
but as more in the street joined in, they clapped
louder and louder as if they were freeing
something within, perhaps a patient who never
had such a chance to applaud the ones
who nursed them when they were ill.

Everyone was clapping all over the country
banging lids, pots. Fireworks lit the sky.
Their spirits zoomed. They felt how a patient
must feel when administered good news.
Their hands will never finish clapping.
Everyone has been a patient.
Everyone's hearts are clapping.
As long as hearts clap, hands will too.

OWEN GALLAGHER, London

THE GUIDANCE

The first text shocked me. We have identified that you
are at risk of severe illness if you catch coronavirus.
Please remain at home for a minimum of 12 weeks.
Home is the safest place for you. Wash your hands more
often, for at least 20 seconds. And there is more .
Ask your family, friends or neighbours to collect your
prescriptions. Do you live with others? Stay 3 steps away.
Sleep separately. Sex is unwise. Check you have vegetables,
dry food and soap. Prepare for hospital, get a single bag
ready with essentials for an overnight stay. My essentials
seem out of place, book, notebook, change of clothes.
I've watched hospital admissions. A single bag would be
wasted. I could click to unsubscribe, but it's compelling.
We watch news at six. At 10, it feels terrifying. 900 dead
in one day, in Italy. O! Italy, land of my eighteenth year,
sun and sand. The Guidance has changed to Notifications.
Yesterday we exceeded our one hour's exercise, tramping
the woods, whistling and whooping for a dog that took off,
nose down, tearing through the trees. She could hear us
but had a desperate mission of her own. She came home,
exhausted. Last night we chopped wild garlic into a pan,
fried potato cakes. We're running out of salt. I dreamt
I was kidnapped in a steel van, weeping. Babylon Berlin.
You said you'd kidnap me if you could. This morning's text
asks me to learn something new, like sudoku. I hate numbers,
though I am an anxious counter. I count to 50 whilst I'm
foaming soap on my hands. Singing seems far too jolly.
Paula Radcliffe says she counts when she runs.
This feels like a marathon. Not all of us will make it. Sun lured
my magnolias into blossom, a wild cream magnificence of Spring.
The night frost burnt them. Now trees of brittle toffee warn,
too much too soon. My hands are split, cracked and stained
with turmeric. Tonight, I plan nettle soup, picked with gloves on
and boiled for twenty seconds to kill the sting.

ANN GRAY, Cornwall

INVADER'S SONG

I do not mean to offend.
I only want to connect.
I want you to be my friend.
At first you will not suspect
I'm anywhere near. You'll feel
Fine – not remotely wrecked.
I'll find your Achilles' heel.
I enter unannounced,
a concept, and yet for real.
I'll be the ball that bounced
along your inner routes.
Sometimes you'll have me trounced;
at other times the fruits
of my labours will be revealed
and I'll soldier on with a brute's
presence that can't be healed.
Yet I'm only a form of life
and all life with a fate is sealed
as sure as with bullet or knife.
So whether you're living alone
or whether you're husband or wife
I will drill through tissue to bone
and on to coffin or urn
in their silent twilight zone.
And if I'm buried or burn
the end is always in sight:
yours and mine. We'll earn
our passage to endless night.

PAUL GROVES, Somerset

GEOFFREY CHAUCER CLEANS THE BEACH

Whan the temperature in June is hotte
Than longen folk to doon what they should notte
And specially from every shire's ende
Of Engelond to Bournemouthe they wende.

Some had woken with the lark
To finde a space where they could parke
Otheres parken everywhere
Legal or not, they did not care

And loutes imbiben swich liquor
Of which vertú engendred is the boor
And disputheth eche hir beachside space
And one anothere puncheth in the face

Then when al that motley bunch were gonne
Cleanen we the beche anon
And finden underwear and socks
And defecations in a box

And so was I seke of hem everichon
That I wrote to my PM anon
To demaunde new laws straight be doon
But from him answere was there noon.

                                                                        JILL HADFIELD, New Zealand

LOCKDOWN LIBRARY

Closed is the building where I once
pounced on William and Billy Bunter, where
The Secret Garden and *The Railway Children*
were stamped out, that for years
has intrigued me with modern novels.

Now is the time for re-reading
the Classics from my shelves.
(I'll shun Camus, Defoe, Marquez.)
It's heroines that come to mind:
of course the Brontë and Eliot women
but also Hardy's Tess and Bathsheba.
It seems the Victorians favoured females
but then I remember Dickens and his
complex, vulnerable young men.

Move on through the years and shelves:
there's Drabble and Murdoch,
Country Girls, Girls of Slender Means,
American Rabbit, Portnoy, Gatsby.

Grouped together are peerless Penguins
with their three horizontal bands,
dubious Eric's Gill Sans font,
their colour-coded classifications:
dominant general orange, criminal green,
adventurous cerise, dark and blue biographies,
purple belles-lettres, dramatic red,
worldly grey, miscellaneous yellow
and the striking, black Modern Poets.

Ah, as well as a lockdown library,
I now have my zoom background.

ALICE HARRISON, Rhyl, Denbighshire

ATHENS, 430 BC.

Plague fell on Athens in the second year
of the Peloponnesian War like
a thunderbolt hurled by angry Zeus.

When Spartans attacked the countryside
farmers abandoned olives and vines
and fled for safety to Athens where they found

disease had ravaged the city. In the agora
where men once strolled discussing philosophy
in fragrant pine-shade beside the temple

bodies were heaped like scythed wheat.
Soon the farmers succumbed; no one
was spared – rich or poor, artist,

soldier, doctor, baker, poet.
*No human art or science was of any
help at all* Thucydides wrote.

Funerals, for those who had someone
to bury them, were quick and quiet;
most Athenians died unwept, unsung.

Nothing protected the great city
or its citizens crowded under the Acropolis.
The historian caught the plague himself.

He had seen what war could do
but groped for words to say *what seemed
too much for human beings to endure*

*people felt a burning in their heads;
their mouths bled; their voices grew
hoarse as crows; their chests ached*

worse was the thirst no water could quench,
a fever so fierce they couldn't bear
clothing to touch their skin; some leapt

naked into water hoping for relief.
In despair Thucydides tells us, the people
turned against Pericles, but their leader

was a man who knew how to handle
a hostile crowd. *I know that war*
and now plague have taken the heart

out of you, he told them. *Just realise*
that the Spartans will go, plague will pass –
you'll still be citizens of a great city.

GAIL HOLST-WARHAFT, Cornell University

NOW, WHAT NEWS ON THE RIALTO?

Silence
a few pigeons
peck at crumbless paving

sickness shades the canal
keeping itself
to itself

a harsh wind
scrapes the shop fronts
whisks up dust

then a marvel
La Fenice* rebuilt song by song
from a hundred windows

                              JOY HOWARD, Kendal

* La Fenice (The Phoenix): the Venice opera house restored after being destroyed by fire three times in its history.

THOUGHT FOR THE DAY

Jesus, here we go, a carpet-slippered tone
shoehorning God into the lack of loo roll;
soft religion, scripted, breathing still,
mock-tender, like a stalker on the phone
persuasive only to itself. The vicar,
imam, rabbi come to call, up-close,
and personal, in emperor's new clothes
of comfort, naked when exposed to rigour.

Creeping slowly over us. Cold flesh.
That was Thought For The Day – a living death –
now wash your hands, face-mask the radio.
There's no vaccine for true believers' lies.
Stay safe! Imagine it's the last thing you
will hear before the ambulance arrives.

KEITH HUTSON, Halifax

WATCHING

I sleep, now, with open curtains
like I did as a child watching
Orion on those breath-tight
sleep-lost nights, watching
the belt, the sword, the silver
shield pushing, pushing
the sky past my window's frame
forever holding the scorpion at bay.

Nights are again breath-tight and sleep-lost.
The stars are missing, only the moon
blurs by. Age has become a blindfold.

We are sleeping in separate rooms.
But I can still feel your breath
on the nape of my neck, your hand
warm on my hip, your absence
my shield.

Lesley Ingram, Ledbury

'I THINK OF THOSE WHO FELL BIZARRELY SILENT'

I think of those who fell bizarrely silent:
Sibelius grand and speechless in Järvenpää,
who descended so quietly toward the grave:
decades-sedentary, in private tinker
with an outline. He would rest considerate
of the truer music which lies always at the gates
of the ear. Neither timid nor brave,
he was suspended in the shape of an endeavour.

I think of those who fell bizarrely silent:
Rimbaud, running guns in Africa,
his letters bare of poetry. He seems,
in each bald missive, an improbable imposter
on the self that could construe *Seasons of Hell*:
and gave himself over to the commercial
as if trying to forget what was hard to redeem:
London and Verlaine: the unbreathable disaster.

I think of those who fell bizarrely silent:
Shakespeare, with gianthood secreted in New Place,
where autograph-hunters never craved to go:
departed neither in glory nor disgrace
quiet about poetry and family feud,
neither validated nor misconstrued –
as if in wintertime he only knew
or cared to think of death's last grace.

I think of all these as our silence lasts
and augments, and changes as it grows:
I think of the power lodged in restraint,
how the high deed is always juxtaposed
with waiting, the huge wonder of a pause.
We need not always have a claim or a cause –
but may stand at death's foothills without complaint
and discharge in peace the burdens of the snow.

CHRIS JACKSON, London

A DROP IN TEMPERATURE

My new man's watching birds through his binoculars
– black cap, fire-crest – as they crisp into view
along with seas of a nearly ripe white moon,
but I'm seeing the blue wings of sorrow,
blurred from weeping and too little sleep.
Cross the stream where it is shallowest, they say,
and soul after soul is crossing now while the tide
is out, so many souls rosaries can't tell
quick enough, even archangels struggle to keep up.
Titles mean nothing now – wifelets, estates –
nor will the arms of the kissing-gate let
anyone back through. It helps me, though,
to think of them as birds, these souls rising
in their thousands from solitary beds,
murmurations huddled in reeds of the afterlife
as they shelter each other from the unexpected drop
in temperature, land in pairs or handfuls
on telegraph wires, share how it was.

ROSIE JACKSON, Devon

SHE DIED ALONE

Belly Mujinga, 1972-2020

She died there in hospital
no husband, Sissy, daughter Ingrid
no church kin around her
and at her funeral of regulation 10
her own Lusamba saw the coffin
and could not imagine her within.

She was a mother to everyone
who was blown into Victoria station
lost for food or direction,
took them home like injured creatures
fed them till they were strong
watched them fly, never to return.

The concourse deserted like Christmas Eve
only without the straggling drunkards
or last-minuters wandering homewards,
when a man cursed and spat hatred
announcing that he had Covid
(though he later tested negative).

She'd worked all hours overtime
to send money home to her mother;
they made her work without PPE
sickness made her vulnerable to disease.
She died alone, the banners remember
outside her station chants of – 'Justice for Belly Mujinga!'

MIKE JENKINS, Merthyr Tydfil

IN TIME OF PLAGUE

Simple. You whip the egg and grate the cheese
Chop basil melt some butter in the pan
Pour wait and fold. Warmed plate when you began
Buttered some bread and made a choice of teas.
Perhaps an apple. How we spend our days
Waiting for ends that may or may not come.
Something so small may summon with the thumb
It does not have. And meanwhile music plays
I change the disc Tchaikovsky and then Bach
And work a little. It is spring outside
Sun on my balcony. Last night I cried
For all we lose. Wrote an unkind remark
Thought better. Work. I must resist regret
For things done, things undone. There is time yet.

Roz Kaveney, London

COVID NIGHTS

to Gillie, Tim, Matthew

3am - no cars, no moon, no stars, no cat yowls,
no dog howls, only this clear voice which asks
'On whose walls will these pictures hang,
where will four thousand books find home, who
will dust my mother's Staffordshire, her Spode,
Crown Derby, Famille Rose, Meissen figurines?'

Lying here, only one thing's sure - when I go,
which may be soon, I'll no longer know nor care.

Angela Kirby, London

A GRANDMOTHER PREPARES FOR LOCKDOWN

The day they last met, air was sharp and pale,
but gentle on bare arms, while far below a sail
breezed out of sight. They kept beyond touch,
obedient to advice which could be borne, much
like an April shower, no wounding barrage of hail.

They wore brave smiles, promised without fail
to meet again. But granite cliffs turned to shale
no toeholds, handfuls of grass too scant to clutch,
the day after they last met.

Toys and books tidied away, she tried to nail
down voices, memories that would not go stale
small hands resting in hers, erased the smutch
of squabbles. Unclipping booster seats, such
bleak sorrow whelmed, swept sobs into a wail
for the day they last met.

CAMILLA LAMBERT, Arundel, West Sussex

Hungry for touch?
Please contact
the relevant bodies.

JOHN LANYON, Charlbury, Oxfordshire

APPLAUSE

For carers, of course. But let us not forget the chaps
in day-glo vests who empty bins, steer street-sweepers between
parked cars, fill holes in roads and repaint worn white lines.

And hats off too to bus drivers and train drivers; the folk
who bring us bills and birthday cards; winged messengers
who ring and run, leaving parcels on the step.

Give thanks to the courageous souls who save the lives
of capsized crews, and swimmers caught in undertow; who rescue
cats from lofty trees, cut bodies from wrecked cars, extinguish fires.

Remember warehouse employees who pick goods bought
with PayPal clicks; the shelf-fillers and checkout staff
and everyone who marshalls us in well-spaced queues.

Let's raise a glass to three-star chefs who sweat producing meals
for health professionals, and teams who toil through storm
and drought to grow and harvest vegetables and fruit.

Praise be to every engineer who sets up kit for those who sit
at mics in bedrooms, studies, sheds, with reverb
duvet-damped, providing soundtracks to our days.

In virtual choirs, from pavements, balconies and lawns
let's raise our hallelujahs to them all.

GILL LEARNER, Reading

A GUINEA-PIG'S SUSPICIONS

The mayor is shocked when a local lockdown in Leicester
is announced. No forewarning. Local authority figures pester
for data, not released for another week. The Leicester Mercury
lists the top ten areas with the highest cases in the city,
small industrial units cramped in areas of high density
housing, multi-generational households; and requests clarity.

In an information vacuum, social media ramps up uncertainty.
Frustration lashes out. Racism rears its ugly head. New delay:
5pm announcement done at 9.15pm. Leaks say easing for the city
will be delayed. More leaks: lockdown extended to city/county
borders: Oadby, Birstall, Glenfield, map promised *imminently*.
Full briefing tomorrow. Dawn brings grey cloud rather than clarity.

I drive out to do my weekly supermarket shop, not knowing
if I cross a boundary between lockdowns. The bunting thanking
NHS and keyworkers sags. A magpie lies in the road, no
visible injury. Stiffened feathers don't react to the breeze. Two
refuse to lie flat, their vanes disturbed and separated.
The shop's cleaner is wearing her mask again. It was junked
last week. Unpacking my shopping, it's quiet enough to hear
a neighbour's guinea pig squeal. It's woken and moved near
its food bowl where it baulks at a fresh treat of savoy
cabbage. A change in its routine might be some form of trickery.

EMMA LEE, Leicestershire

DEATH LEAVES A MESSAGE – MAYBE

A man's voice muddy as coffee-grounds
mutters in the answerphone:
I try over and over to make out what he wants
but the words coagulate.
Weeks into lockdown
maybe it's Death, who's close now
(he came for my two friends,
nightly snatches hundreds) – but who
in this house is his message for, which one?
Let it not be me, not yet.
Let it be me.

                                      Pippa Little, Newcastle upon Tyne

VISITING MUM AT CHRISTMAS

For my daughter – April 3rd 2020

On Christmas Eve in 1987,
half way through a bowl of mushroom soup in Debenhams,
    Bournemouth,
I realised I couldn't carry on,

took to my bed that night with flu and didn't get up for 14 days,
apart from lying on the rear seat of the Ford Orion
for the 320 mile journey home to Saltburn.

Another two weeks and a stone lighter.

That Christmas Day, my Mum took umbrage,
'I've been to all this trouble. Surely you can manage a little dinner.'

I think I might be pregnant changed her tune.
She called the doctor out. She had a track record.
Seven months later, the baby boy was fine.

It's Day 12 for my daughter: still no sense of taste or smell,
total exhaustion, a breathy voice. She's lost the cough
and never had the fever. And she's miles away in London.

Missing my Mum, who called the doctor out on Christmas Day in
    1983
when I was first pregnant: excruciating stomach pains,

he diagnosed as indigestion.   Come on my Girl
get better soon. You, who were born in Whitby Hospital
at the height of the miners' strike. Come on fighter,

beat the Covid Bastard.

                                          MARILYN LONGSTAFF, Darlington

VIOLET CARPENTER BEE: SPRING 2020

A big black Bee against my window pane
Crackles with rage, struggling in vain
In wild frustrated agony to pass
The inexplicable block of glass.

The window's stuck. But I open wide
The big glass patio door, and guide
My winter tenant to the spring outside.

She circles once, then seems to hesitate –
Then sallies forth to feed and pollinate.
And I feel honoured to have set her free,
Essential worker for humanity.
When hierarchy breaks down in the hive,
Only the wild Bee keeps the world alive.

Carpenter Bee, brought to these northern climes
By a warming planet, in perilous times;
Violet Carpenter Bee, whose wings change hue
In sunlight to a dark translucent blue.

Wild flowers unfold for her their nectar treasure;
All nature wakes to labour that is pleasure;
Birds build their nests in budding trees and sing --
With gold-dust glistening on leg and wing,
From flower to flower my Bee goes visiting,
Oblivious to social distancing.

But while I set my Bee at large to roam,
Mankind immobilised remains at home.
A microbe holds humanity in thrall
Behind a baffling and invisible wall.

Lockdown will end one day, when they will find
A vaccine or a cure; but can mankind
Defeat the pathogen within the mind,
And, breaking man-made walls and distancing,
Experience at last the human spring?

DEBORAH MACCOBY, Leeds

FIRST WALK OUT ALONG CALDON CANAL

I thought it might look changed, but it's the same
old fallen world out here — the shifting sky
keeps shifting, thick with rain. We play a game
along the bank — that people passing by
are dead celebrities, pale ghosts of fame.
There's Elvis, see? Off to the shop to buy
essential peanut butter (who could blame
the King for this indulgence now? Not I).

A drone flies by. You shiver, button your coat
and check your watch, anxious about the rules,
the news, the air. Three ducklings weave and float
through scum and leaves, the oily rainbow pools
that gather by the locks. A moored canal boat
creaks and rocks. *Queen Mum's inside! Right fools*
she thinks we are. The past seems so remote.
She's swigging gin and rattling her jewels.

And look! There's Philip Larkin in his mac!
Swaggering along with a stick, content at last,
no social calls to make, no books to stack.
I take your hand. The sky is overcast
and the world is trying to shake us off its back.
It's time we went. And suddenly the past
is clamouring with countless dead, and black
and empty space ahead — still and vast.

      MARK MCDONNELL, Leek, Staffordshire

THEY SAY THE LAST COLOUR WE SEE IS BLUE

in remembrance of all who have died from Covid 19

Before the light went
what did you think of?

Indigo, caerulean,
cobalt, marine, navy,
the artist's catalogue of blues?

African skies,
the clear blue cross on the Finnish flag,
purple-blue of Irish hills,
the blue of Gougane Barra's lake?

Or the perfect blue
of the small forget-me-not,
its yellow eye a sun,
its name a plea?

GILL McEVOY, Devon

I'M SORRY THIS POEM IS LATE BUT I'VE HAD COVID 19

for the past six months. Mildly,
which is bad enough. All of
the symptoms sequentially:
hand pain, headaches, loss of taste,
gastric attacks, dizziness, weakness—
everyone knows them now.

There were scary days,
days I'd stand up and fall
straight back down, days
the world felt furry because my lungs
felt furry and incorrectly buttressed

Sometimes I remember to eat
even without appetite though
the new sense of taste prefers
sweet things. But I cook healthy meals
then let them go off in the fridge
because brain fog blurs them
into two weeks ago.

Anyway, yes. So this is late.
By the way, it mixes
really fucking badly
with perimenopause.

Just so you know.

JENNIFER A. MCGOWAN, Didcot, Oxfordshire

TEN HILLSBOROUGHS

Ten Hillsboroughs today.
Two 9/11s since we started counting.
And that's just the hospitals:

bodies will be lying now in flats,
awaiting their discovery
which could be days or weeks

or months away. There will be houses,
care homes, yet to be discovered.
I scroll my feed and wonder

who I've not seen for a while.
I talk with my mother each day,
saying not much more than yes,

I'm still alive. On that day in September,
I messaged a friend trapped in Reykjavik.
We grew apart before the days

of total connectivity: I wonder how he's
doing now. Ten Hillsboroughs.

Near half a dozen Hungerfords.

And the headline is a man
has watched Love Actually.

Anathema Jane McKenna, Newcastle upon Tyne

708 TODAY

That's fewer than yesterday
and the day before.
It sounds encouraging,
unless, of course, the 708th
was someone you loved.

My brother, for instance,
has for the last fortnight been
unconscious on a ventilator,
so in a way one might almost say
he died two weeks ago

except he didn't. He was still there,
cared for by skilled medical staff,
and from day to day, hope rose
and fell in us like the oxygen
being pumped in and out of his lungs.

He had a name, a history, was unique,
has been part of my identity
since the day that I was born.
This makes it all the harder now to accept
his new status as a national statistic.

ALWYN MARRIAGE, Guildford

A RIVERSIDE WALK IN TIMES OF COVID

Picking my way round stinging nettles
and the purple flowers of deadly nightshade,
I watch as a large white butterfly settles
in a patch of great willow-herb.

In the river, two long-necked swans
glide past with brown-plumed cygnets.
'Here, duckies, duckies!' shouts a toddler, and dons
a t-shirt thrown off in the August heat.

All peaceful: a bucolic scene within a city park.
But among the masked and unmasked families
the coronavirus has left its mark
in tales of those who've caught it; not survived.

DEBORAH MASON, Oxford

COOKING IN A TIME OF LOCKDOWN

Start with the herbs. The sage and thyme.
Pick lavender and pansy, columbine,
bay leaves and fennel, mint and lemon balm.

Perhaps tonight a delicate parsnip wine,
salad of bittercress, sweet violet, chicory,
damson and apple tansy, eggs in moonshine.

And in these times of empty cupboards,
the scrimp-and-save of living thriftily, I turn
to older ways. Walk lanes and meadows

searching for hoards of nettles, strawberries,
filling my bag with elderflower, foraging
wild chamomile and soft red raspberry.

I remember days of bread-and-dripping,
scrag-end or scraps, meals that had to last.
Broths of ox-tail, bowls of chitterlings.

My mother's books are faded now, passed
down through generations, each recipe a spell
cast by her fingers into a tempting feast.

I see her, apron pockets always full
of hair-clips, chocolate biscuits, wooden pegs.
Taste the home-made macaroons, smell

the new-baked bread. Sponge cake waisted
with plum jam, plates piled high with scones.
A hug of battenberg in almond paste.

I think of her as I rummage in my fridge
for cream, a nub of lard, an ounce of butter,
sift the flour to make a blackberry pie.

And in this kitchen, warm with memory,
we stand together rolling out our dreams.

KATHY MILES, Aberaeron

OUT WALKING

*If you see me coming
better step aside.*

*A lot of men didn't
and a lot of men died . . .*

Out walking now
I remember this song

as I measure my distance
not to avoid death

but to help save lives.
See me perfect my neighbourly

swerve and dip
away from the pavement

or my deft parabola
when exercising in the park,

part virtue, part apology,
and always with a smile.

JOHN MOLE, St Albans

SEA PARK, WEYMOUTH

Our bay is home to several gaudy floating palaces these days.
Nobody wants to cruise the world just now, in Covid times.
These are plague ships: people took sick on them and died
early on in the pandemic – ocean-going hotels become death traps,
denied access to ports. So it continues. Skeleton crews
are trapped aboard, like Davy Jones, condemned to sail on
in sight of land, their hearts ashore: themselves in purdah.

All day the ships lie sullen in our mighty bay. Sometimes they sound
a mournful klaxon of farewell, and head into the Channel
on their way to Falmouth, Teignmouth or Southampton.
It's only busy work, to keep their engines ticking over.
Then back they come to stand again aloof out in the bay,
noses in air, high out of the water (being empty of all but ghosts).

Local pleasure boats run tours around the towering hulls.
The skippers do their homework: pointing out the mighty liner
Queen Elizabeth. See her maids-in-waiting moored beside her:
Britannia; Allure, Jewel, Explorer and Anthem of the Seas -
four seasick sisters with nothing now to do but gossip with each
    other.
Marella lifts her anchor and heads west, but she'll be back tomorrow.
She's gone to join Queen Mary in Torbay. Just a walk to stretch her
    legs.

Each ship wears a little pall of smog: a diesel exhalation
that in high pressure weather we can taste deep in our throats.
Their klaxons sound like fog horns used on thick nights in my youth
decades before satnav, and other modern aids to navigation.
At night their lights blaze out across the bay, reminding us
of their presence in our lives. They are a fixture. Here for the duration.

We have grown fond of them. Or tolerant at least.
I count them every evening as their lights come on out in the bay.
Then looking down I find that this has been, for me, another PJ day.

                                      JUDI MOORE, Weymouth

THE MEETING

I met three neighbours on the road
Just as I used to do.
We backed away, we stood apart
To let the virus through.

I saw the virus in my mind.
It hung there like a pall.
It cast a shadow deep and long
Which reached the ivied wall.

The shadow moved, but we were still.
The shadow moved between.
The shadow had its own dark strength
For it was cold and mean.

I shivered to my bones and shrank
Into my fearful mind.
My words had stopped. The shadow touched
All it could reach or find.

My neighbours fled but I stood still,
My feet fixed to the road.
I could not budge. It was as if
I struggled with a load.

My voice had gone. I could not shout.
All words were strangled now.
The shadow stole my voice from me
And only it knew how.

An eerie wind began to blow
Among the quaking trees.
I saw the grass, and it was bent
By this unearthly breeze.

The clouds turned black, the thunder came,
The oak trees flashed and bowed.
My body was struck down. I lay
With branches as my shroud.

In death I joined the thousands dead
Who lay in silent rooms.
No mourners came to see the throng
Of corpses without tombs.

The dead rose up and slowly moved
Along a Cornish lane.
There was no dirge, there were no hymns.
It all began again.

I met three neighbours on the road
Just as I used to do.
They backed away, they stood apart
To let the virus through.

Lucy Newlyn, Cornwall

GRETA'S WISH

History often gives us clues —
how is it that we never guessed?
The parallels were there to see:
an unseen killer from the East
took hold in Europe, quickly spread
to soon storm London's crowded streets.
And why were lessons never learnt
on isolating travellers? —
So easy for an island race...

Back then, the King and Courtiers fled.
Today, Range Rovers all left town
leaving the city looking dead
and ordinary folk locked down.
The growing deaths, shortage of food
were common to both then and now
with doctors in strange masks and gowns —
today, they could have come from Space,
in sixty-five they looked like birds.

Back in King Charles the Second's time
foul air, *miasma*, took the blame.
Fresh herbs were held next to each nose,
fires were lit and people smoked
to help protect them from the Plague.
More false science made people think
that plague was spread by cats and dogs,
a cull was made of family pets
while the real culprits, rats, got off.

Four centuries on, not much has changed
except for our technologies...
Still strange beliefs proliferate
with social media full of fools
who push quack medicine as cures

and blame 5G for current woes
(as if a virus could be spread
by changes to telephony!)
Yet, lack of planning let us down...

The Plague died back, The Fire came
and London was rebuilt again…
Perhaps the outcome from our storm
will change the World, spark Greta's flame?

King Charles (1630 – 1685); The Great Plague1665 -66; The Fire of London 1666

PATRICK OSADA, Berkshire

DOMINIC CUMMINGS PREPARES FOR HIS TRIP

for Mel

I saw you waving a safety helmet and thought -
here is a man who cares about collisions to his children
here is a man who wore a seat belt to be safe on journeys.
I have a friend who is on a journey of depression right now
she has not seen her Mum in a care home for two months,
long ago when pregnant her waters kept her baby safe
for nine months her body was a care home built of DNA bricks
she raised them in the whole wide world of their tiny universe.
They would set the table to eat together attempting etiquettes.
When they had kids of their own, they got pissed up sometimes
and even then, a mother will give her last paracetamol to her kin.

I picture Dominic Cummings buying the Range Rover he
    journeyed in,
I imagine the order of his questions:
"Do you know who I am"?
"How many speakers does this baby have then"?
"Will you throw in the leather trim"?
"How fast does it go"?
"Oh yes I almost forgot, how many airbags does it have?"
"oh yes, I almost forgot, what is the safety rating of this bad boy"?
"Throw in the tinted windows and we've a deal"
"What kind of commission do you get for one of these"?
"Oh yes, you're not a raging leftie are you"?

I saw a picture of two gloved hands joined of a son and his dying father.
It makes me think how a lifetime of closeness ends with forced distance,
and I want to write "Cunt" on the windscreen of a politician's dustless car,
I want to write a haiku in the covid cremated ashes that cover politicians' cars.
I want to do this very much but am respecting rules written in commoners' blood.
I am listening to a Viking song of a warrior who asked to be buried with his treasure
This treasure was the white hair of his mother so he could join her in Valhalla,
he wanted to say he died a good death but what do we say when we get there?
We are all sons of warriors that invaded and Covid has no honour when it gets in.

ANTONY OWEN, Coventry

EXERCISE

I have tried Pushups off the wall
and *You will need a chair for this*
looking straight ahead raise your leg
sideways - hold - and lower slowly
and now breathe - Arms up! Arms down! Arms
straight through the window pane. La chair
est triste et j'ai lu tous les livres
and I've had - how I've had - TV.
So this evening I managed Out,
and I must thank the two young blokes
chattering up behind who shot
past either side of me, shoulders
almost touching, when the whole road
was empty: and that has made all
the difference. What happened? I yelled.
I yelled so hard that they staggered.
Mumbled *Sorry Ma'am* and scarpered,
while sound that streamed from the bottom
of my cracked lungs astonished me -
round Chaucerian abuse - *Fatheads!*
Nincompoops!
       The sun still shining,
no one in sight, me brandishing
my stick like Sir Adrian Boult
at the Proms, exhilarated.
Somebody tell the BBC:
Yelling is the best exercise.

                          M.R. PEACOCKE, Barnard Castle

BECAUSE THERE WERE NO WOMEN IN THE 'WAR ROOM'

Because there were no women in the war room they thought it was possible to work from home and homeschool your children

Because there were no women in the war room they forgot to count the women killed by their partners in their predicted death toll

Because there were no women in the war room the women and children already in the shelters went hungry as there were no more donations

Because there were no women in the war room the mothers cried with their hungry babies when they could find no formula milk in London

Because there were no women in the war room the female nurses found their protective masks were a men's size small and did not fit them

Because there were no women in the war room the female scientists worried the vaccine trial data would not be separated by gender and would not therefore measure women's different immune reaction

Because there were no women in the war room, it was called a war room

MEGAN PEEL

The good Lord gave us Sunshine,
Then the good Lord gave us Rain.

We gave back Global Warming -
(We were driving Him Insane).

So, He made Corona Virus,
To make us Think Again.

CLIVE PERRETT, Chelmsford

DAY 60

I used to think I was an early riser,
but she's here when I wake up
staring me in the face like I can't see her.

She leans on my shoulder when I'm writing,
imitates me on the phone, follows me

into the sitting-room, lies on the sofa
as if she belongs here, and she thinks
it's all right to interrupt my reading.

I leave her at home when I go to the beach.

She doesn't know how silver sand curves
beside the sea for miles, reflecting blues,
how no one else is here, and I can stand

at the edge of the waves in the wind
breathing out to indigo on the horizon.

As soon as I get back, she's beside me,
when I take off my boots, when I hang up
my coat, when I wash my hands at the sink.

She opens the white wine well before six,
and makes me stay up until after midnight,
which I would never normally do.

No one seems to know how long
she will be staying, and I'm afraid to ask.

The wet windy grey days are the worst.

    PAULINE PRIOR-PITT, Island of North Uist, Outer Hebrides

MEAT MARKET

"He had to hunt and fish during the war in occupied France. He had to shoot his starving dog." Alison Moyet of her father.

Last month this would have been a detail,
something that happened in the war,
in the past, something that made you say,
'What a shame, how sad' – but now it goes deeper
and you look at your pet - already you're imagining
an empty cupboard, are there fish in the canal?

You remember the end of the war, no meat,
Uncle Jim and Uncle Henry going out
in the night to get pigeons from
round Bobby Peel's statue – Uncle Jim couldn't,
so Uncle Henry wrung their necks
and Uncle Jim put them in the sack.

They cut off any ringed legs
and threw them in the fire.
I watched as Uncle Jim sat on a stool
and plucked them, helped him to stuff
the grey feathers into the sack on a nail
behind the scullery door.

There were rabbits on the market,
Aunty Annie insisted on one with a head
in case it was a cat.
And now the small market animals –
the bats, the snakes and the pangolins
are wreaking their terrible revenge.

RITA RAY, Lymm, Cheshire

Rita died in November 2020

KIT

The masks are coming down over the Hindu Kush
into the Oxus valley, the cradle of the world,
on packhorse and steppe pony. Masks made
in sweatshops by tiny flexible fingers on overtime,
their fitted snouts and elasticated earloops
biodegradable, delivered to an outlet near you.

The test-kits are coming to your local drive-in.
Just insert and swab, easy as cleaning your ear.
The test-kits have been tested and found reliable.
All types of delivery available: helicoptered in,
droned down, carried on the backs of robots.
We are working on the app. Watch this space.

The robots are coming to a test-center near you.
Sterilised, speaking in English and other languages.
Just press and hold your forehead near the patch.
No contact necessary. Our latest designer robots
are coming up from the valley to a pass near you
carrying all the kit and caboodle you will need.

PADRAIG ROONEY, Basel, Switzerland

PYROGENIC

> *And the dress… / Branded her soft flesh. Poor girl, / She hurtled up, all fire* – Euripides *Medea*, lines 1183–5, transl. Frederic Raphael and Kenneth McLeish

What reason was there not to adore it,
the dress – its watered silk, its weight;

it shimmered as she moved, silver warp
and rose-pink weft rippling like sunset

on a lake, the fishtail wrapping her ankles.
It clung to her like a second skin, every

mortal cell of her, each pore and hair.
But the dress is hungry, wet turns to fire,

it wants to eat her alive: she melts in its arms,
gum from a blazing pine in the cytokine storm.

LESLEY SAUNDERS, Slough

FOUND POEM FROM *THE EVENING STANDARD*, 8 SEPTEMBER, 2020

OK, so 2020 hasn't been the year that you expected.
Between Covid-induced health anxiety,
job insecurity,
and a general sense of impending doom,
we've felt mentally overburdened for months.
Not to mention there's been no release:
a staycation is no match for a foreign holiday,
and we're all missing parties and blow-out weddings.
Many say they've lost the best part of a year.

You can reclaim a sense of optimism.
Look at things differently.
Try to reconfigure how you look at 2020.
Examine yourself on a personal level
and ask: "Are things really headed in the direction
that feels most aligned for me?"

Look at your biggest fears and boldest desires.
Find yourself a new hobby.
Invest in personal development.
Just don't go in blind.
Feast on culture. Confront money fears.
The Money Is Coming is a new book out.
Plus UK people born 1951-1979
are in for a treat this September.

BRIGHID SCHROER, Oxford

AND NOW THE BEARS

It began with the goats
in the silent streets of Llandudno,
nibbling at window boxes, turning the redundant
roundabout in a children's playground,
and tap-tapping their horns on the empty picture windows
where the tourists used to sit.
Fallow deer soon followed
in the suburbs of Essex,
their dappled backs in the deserted
supermarket carparks, all shyness conquered.
And the usual cats, dogs and foxes
dropped their jaws with astonishment,
knew their moment of urban dominion was finally
over. Next, came the birds,
of every shape and size, across every county,
filling and filling the human vacuum,
singing their loud love songs day and night,
and constructing fantasy nests
in the sweet and soft tranquillity.
As a mark of triumph, a peacock
was even spotted, fanning its tail feathers
in the abandoned streets of Kensington.
And now the bears are at the doors
of the BBC, turning elated in the high-security
turnstiles, testing the hot desks,
roaming the studios, and lumbering heavily
onto The One Show couch,
to finally give voice to the green grass roots
and the really really wild.

ROBERT SEATTER, BBC Broadcasting House: 9 April 2020

THE EFFECT OF SOCIAL DEPRIVATION ON THE DEVELOPMENT OF MONKEY BEHAVIOUR HARLOW, H (1964), PSYCHIATRIC RESEARCH REPORT, VOL 19

After a while, says Monkey, I learned to accept it.
I stopped trying to climb the walls.
Time became malleable
and largely irrelevant.
There's no pressure to sleep at night.

When I find my own pace,
the day is a lake I can float in quite gently.
And the day is incredibly long
and surprisingly busy.
I am a house with many rooms

and the rooms are all filled
with fruit. It's okay to be insane -
some of the visions are pleasant,
my thoughts are extraordinary.
I touch myself very adeptly

and the walls are safety.
It's not as silent as you might expect.
I recite poetry in various forms,
I speak with demons. I am learning
to embrace my own company.

Though lacking resources, I have time.
There's a great deal in here left to learn.

CLARE SHAW, Hebden Bridge

THE CUSTOM OF SHAKING HANDS

That was the year they stopped shaking hands,
the year the porch lights turned green
across the neighborhoods and backstreets
of Kentucky, and someone left roses
on the banks of the Green River
in remembrance of John Prine,
the troubadour of the common man.

That was the year they dug mass graves
in the vacant lots of Central Park,
stacks of plain wooden coffins
filed into the dirt like building blocks
fit together to form an inverse cathedral
to memories best forgot,
and the men in their white plastic suits
and their shovels just kept working,
set to the task of forgetting.

That was the year the famous book stores closed,
the restaurant chairs remained
upside-down on their tables,
their legs like palisades
poised to prevent unwelcome gatherings,
shopping malls, universities, churches
quiet as concrete,
mausoleums to the death of chatter,
the death of congregations,
the death of societal noise.

And the people began to wonder
when they might touch again,
if not to gain assurance
that they were greeted in good faith
without the presence of a gun,
maybe just to feel seen,

acknowledged as more
than another masked participant
in this orgy of the damned,
where every encounter
holds the sustenance of a mime.

JAY SIZEMORE, Portland, Oregon

THIS IS JUST TO SAY (LOCKDOWN)

after William Carlos Williams

I have used up
the toilet roll
that was in
the cupboard

and which
you were probably
hoarding
for an emergency

Forgive me
it was 4-ply
so quilted
and so ultra-soft

PAUL STEPHENSON, Cambridge

IN THE PINK

… who says it these days?

And who, who says it these days,
would say it these last days?

Tantamount to tempting fate.
Inviting fatality.

Viruses and us, battling like each
unique fig and matching wasp,

wasp and fig adapting,
one to defend, the other to conquer,

each trying to keep one step ahead.
You'd think they'd settle for symbiosis,

become friends, cosy up, stop
each forever trying to kill the other.

But what sense talking sense?
There's no reasoning,

not with figs and wasps, viruses.
And what should be said of us?

ANNE STEWART, Orpington

LANDLINE

Last night when the phone rang late, caller ID
said home. But I thought I was home, who is
this please? No one answers. The room is changed,
a space waiting. There's the first light between
the curtains but it's still hours till dawn yet.
I hang up. It keeps ringing. Home calling.
But I have no idea where that is now
and the line dies. Call back. It rings and rings.
There's no answering machine and no voice
and *the caller did not leave their number.*
No matter. If they ring back, and they will,
I'll be here, when and wherever that is.

                                                          SEÁN STREET, Liverpool

THAT TIME REMEMBERED

Something about duty, about going into the sun
As if it was rare; something about not enough
Of basic things, too much information;
A recollection of locks, distance, and crowds
In parks as if they were safer. A sense the young
Were careless, indifferent, as they always are;
The old preparing for what they knew happens;
A time of waiting, as if the air raid sirens

Had just begun, but the shelters hadn't yet
Flung open. Something else, connected to being
Apart, a decision we made to come together,
A grander union, after division bells, local anger;
Seriousness at a level you could hear in a stadium,
But they were shut. The image of someone holding
A pint glass, laughing at the figures on the telly;
Stocking up on boxed sets, brown rice, macaroni;

Wondering if the straps of your mask were right;
That clutching in the chest like holding on
To your last belongings; a gust of fight or flight.
More dying than had to, but that's politics,
A retired nurse leaning over with exhausted fear,
Back for a final act of compromised immunity;
The blue ventilator wheezing, or was that her?
Funerals without mourners, that enclosing year.

TODD SWIFT, London, 22 March 2020

LOCKDOWN YELLOW

In March, throngs of dandelions
gather in the drab winter grass

In April and May, there are buttercups,
gold dust sprinkled over green hillsides

Now, clusters of birds-foot-trefoil
glint among the swaying June grasses

These bright heads, these armies of small suns
In a world where everything changed

And I think of the Incas, the glory of gold,
the sweat of their god in gleaming temples

The horde they kept from Pizarro,
and hid in a mountain somewhere in Ecuador

I think too of the day you came
in your yellow dress to my door

WISTY THOMAS, London

'ROUND OF APPLAUSE'

You are not clapping for the NHS
You're clapping just to make yourself feel nice.
You do not care about the deep distress
You cause, expecting them to sacrifice

Their lives to care for people such as you,
Who go outside to do a conga line.
Who cough and say "I'm sure it's just the flu"
Then pop out to the shop to get more wine.

Till suddenly you find that you can't breathe
Call 111, and then call 999,
And even as you gasp for breath, believe
Those street parties two weeks ago were fine.

Don't stand and clap next Thursday; stay inside.
In ten days, count how many more have died.

SERIN THOMASIN, Sheffield

CONVERSATION WITH THE VIRUS

'So, you're seventy this September, huh?'
'Yeah, but I look and feel younger.'
'And you've prostate cancer?'
'Low level, mate, and currently inactive.'
'And asthma?'
'Not used my inhaler for three years.'
'How come?'
'I'm a full-on fitness freak, Fitbit devotee
And daily disciple of my cross-trainer.'
'You should kick that lot into touch
And act your bloody age, my friend.'
'Why, so you can add me to your death list?'
No reply. The virus merely smiles.

NICK TOCZEK, Bradford

COVID – 19 V THE OUT OF DATE OLIVES

It's an uncomfortable cliché to be creating a pyramid of toilet rolls,
cramming Paracetamol into an already over-crowded bathroom cabinet,
and anxiously counting and re-counting tins of soup and jars of pasta sauce,
while we await a Hobbesian apocalypse and life becoming nasty, brutish and short.

So I decide to do something useful instead and clear out our kitchen cupboards,
to make room for survival supplies, where I find, wedged at the back:

An out- of- date and rather sticky squeezy jar of Bovril he bought once,
saying he'd drink it regularly to improve his iron count. Never opened.

Half a pack of sugar - solid with damp – a reminder of a short-lived foray into baking,
together with some possibly mouse-chewed (how could they get up there?) stale chocolate chips.

A bright yellow plastic container of NesQuick chocolate milkshake powder
that used to come out when the great- nephew came to stay in the school holidays.
He has now upgraded to Shaken Udder salted caramel chocolate milk shake from Waitrose.
He has expensive tastes and we love to spoil him rotten.

Red lentils, which would seem like ideal provisions for lockdown emergencies
except they seem to be moving in the jar. Can you get weevils in lentils? Extra protein?

And a jar of lush green Spanish olives that's six years past its
    use-by date.
That one's down to me. I'm the olive addict. How did it
    escape consumption?

We decide that - in extremis - we would rather gnaw off our
    own arms or eat each other
than risk the olives, so we empty them into the food recycling
    bin. The jar is washed
carefully and also put into the appropriate recycling bin. The
    world as we know it
may be coming to an end but we are not completely feral – at
    least not yet.

Tomorrow I'll clear out the bathroom cabinet and check the
    emergency cyanide
suicide pills are still in place. If not, then the olives may have to
    come back out of the bin.

CHRISTINE VIAL, Enfield

US

Birthrate worldwide is 11,000 babies a minute.

The coronavirus/climate-change double
is triple, it seems; yet Packham alone has
addressed such totals lately.

We need to redirection them
(us) as briefly as possible. No, *not* genocide, mass-killings,
murders –

for that with unfaith must entrap the hope
death loves,

such to kill off finally
the one box evident everywhere
in all this shambles:
human goodness (so some name it).

That rarity too, the abecedary, without which
nothing is Writ, holy or otherwise....

Every babe a celeb. Every corona a star.

                              JOHN POWELL WARD, Dartford, Kent

2019

2019 was the year I discovered stained glass,
got myself inside various chapels and cathedrals,
was awed by the scarlet, azure, emerald, angels,
monsters. But in 2020 the churches closed.

2019 was the year I went knocking on doors
and, for a short time, cherished the hope that we could
get rid of a shameless gang, and be part of Europe.

2019 was the year when I had my last sight
of the sea (in North Bay, Scarborough), and turned my back
reluctantly, wondering if this was my last sight ever.

2019 was the year when my daughter's marriage
seemed solid, the year I implicitly believed
in red roses on Valentine's Day, and smiling children;
more fool I. And now it's the plague year, 2020.

MERRYN WILLIAMS, Oxford

LIMERICK

A virus called Covid-19
Attempted to dine with the queen.
She got all confused,
Said, "We're not amused,
And heaven knows where you have been."

STEPHEN WILSON, Oxford

LOCKDOWN

The mirror captures his
reflection. Honest with
himself (you need no mask
in solitude) he trusts
his own sufficiency.
A single file of days
elapses into months,
the future out of reach.

He has the words, stockpiled
for fear of scarcity,
but dare not draw on them.
They threaten clarity.
Sequestered in himself,
he speaks to nobody.

GREGORY WOODS, Nottingham

THE HAAR

Fog enfolds us at summer's peak.
We might as well be islanded here at the harbour's edge,
waiting for something, god knows what,
to signal over the wall from out of the haar.
This mist has thickened for four days now,
the evening lights remind me of impressionist prints;
when I trudge out in wellies, the dog
runs on, as if we're scouting the out-of-reach
before the inevitable - we beat a retreat
and like all living things are entranced by the fire.
Here it's easy to tell yourself the world's your friend,
everyone's drunk or asleep
and wake to find the bay's last light snuffed out,
the clocks don't count, we're folded within and without,
then tap a screen for latest news, up close
of wars and demons on the approach.

NEIL YOUNG, Stonehaven, Aberdeenshire